ANIMALS OF THE ICE AGE

Contents

WRITTEN AND ILLUSTRATED BY JON HUGHES

CAMBRIDGE
UNIVERSITY PRESS

UCL
Institute of Education

WHAT IS AN ICE AGE?

An ice age is when the **climate** on Earth gets colder and colder. Huge areas are covered with ice and snow. Scientists know that this has happened several times in the history of the Earth, although they don't know why.

Winter in the Ice Age was much longer and colder than it is today.

What happens to the animals in an ice age? Some die, but others find ways of living in the cold. They grow bigger and they also grow thick woolly coats. They develop layers of fat to keep warm.

*Mammoths were able to **survive** in the Ice Age.*

WHAT HAPPENS IN AN ICE AGE?

In an ice age, the ice at the North and South Poles spreads and spreads. Scientists call it an **ice sheet** and it can be nearly five kilometres thick. Rivers of ice, called **glaciers**, slide across the land, cutting through mountains.

The climate on Earth changes in an ice age, even in places where there are no ice sheets. Summers become short and winters are long and freezing.

North America

Europe, Middle East

Australia

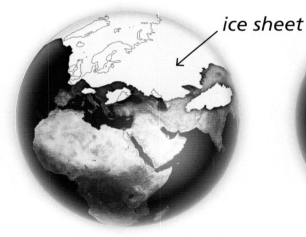
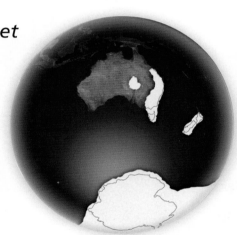

ice sheet

South America

North Africa and Asia

These pictures show how much of the Earth was covered with ice in the Ice Age.

FACT

Ice-age summers were cool. Not all the snow and ice melted.

5

Early humans

If we could go back thousands of years to when the Earth was cooler, what might we see? There were no dinosaurs. They had all died out. We would see many different kinds of animals which had learned to live in the cold. We might also see early humans hunting big grass-eating animals like mammoths, for food.

Early humans learned to survive in the Ice Age.

Mammoths

Mammoths looked rather like elephants today, but they were bigger. They used their long **tusks** for clearing snow, so they could eat the grass underneath. They had two coats – a layer of hair on top and a woolly undercoat.

We know about mammoths because we have found paintings of them in the caves where early humans lived. Scientists have also found the **remains** of mammoths. The biggest mammoth was found in Northern China.

FACT

An adult male mammoth weighed about 6 tonnes.

Its tusks were over 4 metres long.

Mammoths had small tails. This is because a long tail would get frozen in the winter.

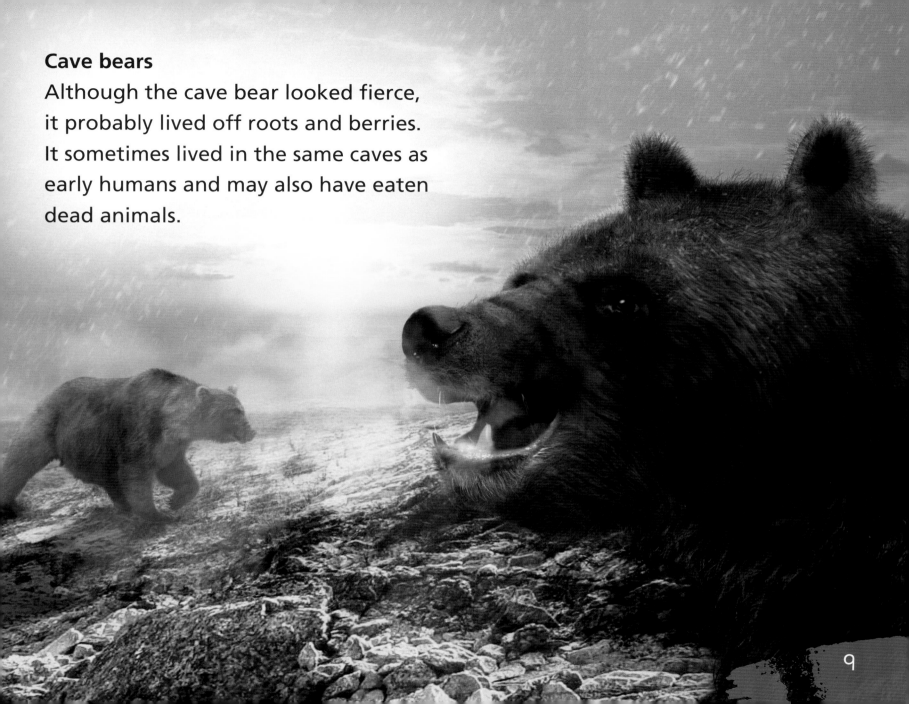

Cave bears

Although the cave bear looked fierce, it probably lived off roots and berries. It sometimes lived in the same caves as early humans and may also have eaten dead animals.

Sabre-toothed tiger

Humans were not the only hunters. The sabre-toothed tiger also ate big grass-eating animals.

FACT

The sabre-toothed tiger was about the size of a modern lion but its two **canine** teeth were nearly 18 cm long.

Smilodon (smile-uh-don)

The most scary of the sabre-toothed tigers was Smilodon. It would hide and leap out on its **prey**. It ate animals much bigger than itself.

Ground sloth

The gigantic ground sloth looked rather like a huge hamster. Humans may have hunted it because it moved slowly. It had sharp claws but it seems to have used them for ripping bark off trees and collecting leaves.

This huge ground sloth was as big as a modern elephant.

Glyptodon (glip-toe-don)

Glyptodon was about the size of a small car. It ate plants and was covered with thick bony plates, even on its head. It needed these plates to keep it safe. Scientists think that Smilodon ate animals like this.

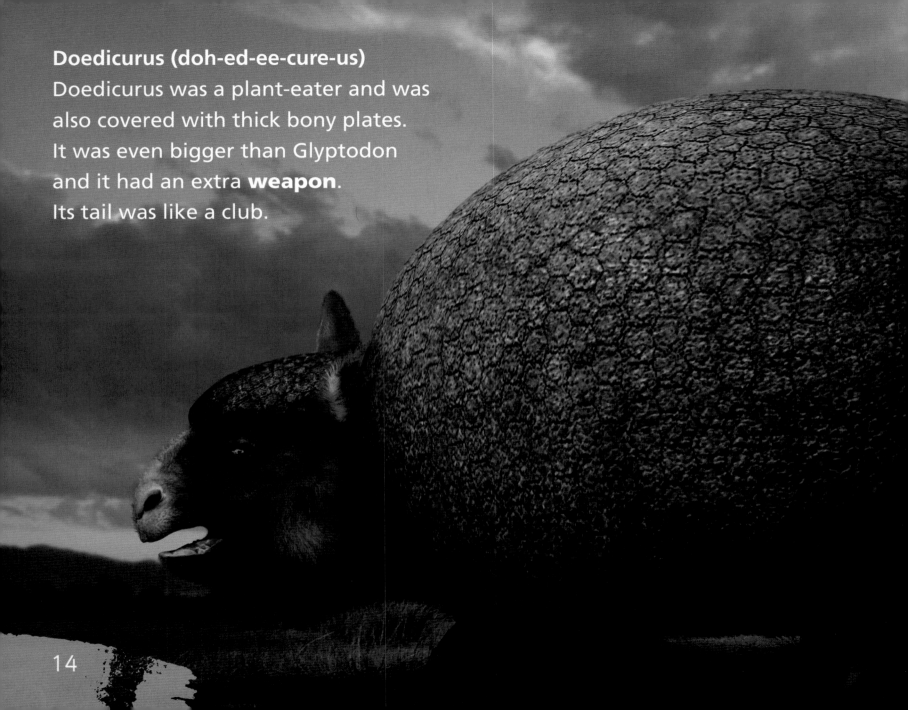

Doedicurus (doh-ed-ee-cure-us)
Doedicurus was a plant-eater and was
also covered with thick bony plates.
It was even bigger than Glyptodon
and it had an extra **weapon**.
Its tail was like a club.

14

Terratorn (terr-ah-torn)

Terratorn was a huge bird of prey which could eat a small animal whole. It could fly great distances.

Not all the world was covered with ice. Most of Australia had no ice and it had many animals. Procoptodon (pro-cop-toe-don) was the biggest kangaroo that ever lived and it ate leaves.

Procoptodon

Diprotodon (die-pro-toe-don)
This animal lived in Australia and carried its babies in its **pouch**.

Thylacoleo (thigh-lah-coe-lee-oh)

This animal lived in Australia. It carried its babies in a pouch like a modern kangaroo, but it ate meat. It was a terrifying hunter about the size of a small lion.

FACT Thylacoleo had huge claws and could climb trees after its prey.

WHAT HAPPENED TO THE ANIMALS OF THE ICE AGE?

Most of the animals from the Ice Age have died out. Scientists call it **extinction**. Scientists think that many ice-age animals died out when the climate became warmer and drier. Since then, many other animals have also died out, like the dodo.

The dodo was a large bird that could not fly. It died out because it could not protect itself from humans.

EXTINCT

Steller's sea cows moved very slowly. It was difficult for them to escape human hunters and they also died out.

EXTINCT

Steller's sea cow

MAYBE EXTINCT

← Tasmanian tiger

Tasmanian tigers were not tigers at all. They were about the size of dogs and most scientists think that they have become extinct.

Today, scientists are finding the remains of extinct animals from long ago. They are finding out how and why these amazing animals died.

Scientists found the remains of a wolf from the Ice Age. It still had a piece of tooth from a sabre-toothed tiger stuck in its **skull**.

Not long ago, scientists dug up a frozen mammoth from the Arctic. They could see what it had looked like. They found out how old it was and they discovered that it ate grass and flowering plants and the bark from trees. Animals in the Ice Age died a long time ago, but scientists are now beginning to learn how they lived.

Mammoths became extinct thousands of years ago.

canine: kind of tooth

climate: expected weather in any place

extinction: when a kind of animal or plant dies out for ever

glaciers: rivers of ice

ice sheet: thick covering of ice over the land

pouch: bag or pocket where animals keep their babies,
for example, kangaroos

prey: animal that is hunted and killed
by another for food

remains: things that are left behind

skull: bones of the head

survive: live

tusks: huge teeth

weapon: something used for attack or defence

INDEX

ANIMALS OF THE ICE AGE ⟜ JON HUGHES

Teaching notes written by Sue Bodman and Glen Franklin

Using this book

Developing reading comprehension

This is a non-fiction report text. It explores how animals of the Ice Age lived, and why they died out. Non-fiction text features, such as sub-headings, fact boxes and diagrams, are included. Captions provide additional information to that given in the main body of the text.

Specialised vocabulary is defined in a glossary. The index can be used to locate specific areas of interest.

Grammar and sentence structure

- Sentences are longer and more complex (e.g. *'We know about mammoths because we have found paintings of them in the caves where early humans lived.'*)

- Commas used to punctuate sentences with dependent (subordinate) clauses (e.g. *'If we could go back thousands of years to when the Earth was cooler, what might we see?'*).

Word meaning and spelling

- There is opportunity to reinforce word-reading skills on unfamiliar words and technical vocabulary.

- Understanding of new vocabulary is supported by the glossary and the non-fiction text features, such as labels and captions.

Curriculum links

Geography – Explore the topography of the region in which the children live for evidence of ice age features. How does this compare with regions that were not covered by ice during the Ice Age (flat deserts, rain forests) – see page.4?

Science – Read other reports about mammoths and other ice age mammals, to build on the information provided here.

Learning outcomes

Children can:

- recognize alternative spellings to read longer and more complex words

- make full use of non-fiction layout

- locate and interpret information in non-fiction

- pose questions, and record these in writing, prior to reading non-fiction to find answers.

A guided reading lesson

Book Introduction

Give a copy of the book to each child. Have them read the title and the blurb independently and ask them to predict what they think this text will be about.

Orientation

Ask: *Is this a fiction or an information text?* Establish that it is an information text and ask the children to flick through the book and identify the key features of non-fiction used in the text.

Draw out what the children know already about the animals they can see in the text. Make links with class work in other areas, and to prior reading.

Ask: *What would you like to find out about animals in the Ice Age?* Each child writes a question in their work book, and shares it with the rest of the group. The teacher also writes one.

Preparation

Demonstrate how you might find an answer to your question. Say: *My question is 'Why were mammoths woolly?'* Look first at the contents page. This does not specifically direct the reader to information about mammoths. Turn to the index. Show how the index is arranged alphabetically and look for the pages that are about mammoths (pages 7 and 8). Turn to those pages. Read the text and check if the fact box gives any further information.

NB – the text does not directly state why mammoths were woolly, but it is inferred through the reference to the cold conditions. This will support development of inferential skills.

Turn to page 9. Find the sentence: *'Although the cave bear looked fierce, it probably lived off roots and berries'*. Explore the use of the comma to delineate clauses, and identify the two ideas discussed in